Buck Wilder

Special Softcover Edition
First Edition
First Printing – June 1997

Publisher's Cataloging-in-Publication Data
Author: Smith, Timothy R.
    Buck Wilder's Small Fry Hiking and Camping Guide: a complete introduction to the world of hiking and camping for small twigs of all ages/ by Timothy R. Smith, author and Mark J. Herrick, illustrator — Traverse City, Michigan:
    Alexander & Smith Publishing, © 1997
    64 p. : col. Ill. ; 28 cm.

    Hardcover Edition:
    ISBN: 0-9643793-3-3
    UPC: 7-5324079333-0

    Softcover Edition:
    ISBN: 0-9643793-2-5
    UPC: 7-5324079325-5

    1. Hiking – North America – Juvenile literature 2. Camping – North America – Juvenile Literature
3. Outdoor Recreation – North America – Juvenile Literature I. Title
Illustrator: Mark J. Herrick
GV191.63   1997
796.5   dc20   LCCN 96-095454

10 9 8 7 6 5 4 3 2 1 – First Printing

Our thanks to Patty Corbett for editorial assistance.

Printed in Hong Kong

Buck Wilder books are available for bulk purchase.
For details contact:
    Buck Wilder Books
    4160 M-72 East
    Williamsburg, MI 49690
    (616) 938-3009 or 1-800-994-BUCK
    Fax (616) 938-3263

I'M BUCK WILDER!
I LOVE TO GO...
HIKING AND CAMPING!

Based on my hiking and camping experiences and the wonderful times I've had outdoors, I know that you are going to love this book. This is my guide to enjoying a great outdoor experience. Use it as a guide, have fun with it, and learn from it. This book is written for all you small twigs—no matter the age.

CONTENTS

BASICS FOR HIK...

Pick and choose what you may need depending on whether you are hiking and/or camping, how many overnights are expected, and the type of terrain and weather conditions you will be in.

👉 THE BASICS OF SURVIVAL 👈

FOOD

Salt, Pepper, Spices

PEANUT BUTTER

DEHYDRATED SOUP

- Basic Food Groups
- Portable
- Nutritious

CLOTHING

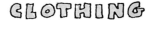

Comfortable Shoes

Rain gear (outerwear)

Undies (clean)

Layered Clothing

- Warm
- Breathable
- Comfortable

SHELTER

Tent

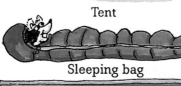

Sleeping bag

- Dependable
- Sturdy
- Protective

EXTRA

NICE TO...

Lantern

Hatchet

Extra Batteries

Portable Burner

Portable Cooking Grill

Rope

RECOMMENDED TO HAVE

Flashlight

Compass

POCKET KNIFE

MATCHES

DRY MATCHES

FIRST AID

Add scissors, rubber bands, wire, mirror, safety pins, needle and thread, and water purification tablets.

BUG OFF

RID ALL

Insect Repellent

SOAP

TOOTH PASTE

Personal Hygiene Kit

Cooking Gear

Towel

TRASH BAGS

I.D.

Wallet

Permits
Licenses
Personal I.D.

Mat

EMERGENCY PACK

Put extra matches, kindling, and paper in a small plastic bag. Put a whistle, money, sunscreen, and sunglasses in there, too!

T.P.

Toilet Paper

STUFF

HAVE

Camera and Film

FILM

Mess Kit

Fishing Gear

SMALL FRY FISHING GUIDE

A Good Book

Extra Clothing

Swimming Suit

FLIES

You can feel the anticipation and excitement just getting ready to go! Double check your equipment to make sure you didn't forget anything and that everything works as expected. If needed, call ahead for information, especially for weather reports. It's a good idea to let someone know where you are going and when you plan to be back.

TRIAL RUN

BACKYARD CAMPING

Take a trial run by sleeping in your own backyard and make it a memorable outdoor event. You can have loads of fun stargazing, cooking over an outdoor grill, and reading bedtime stories under the Milky Way. Don't forget the marshmallows!

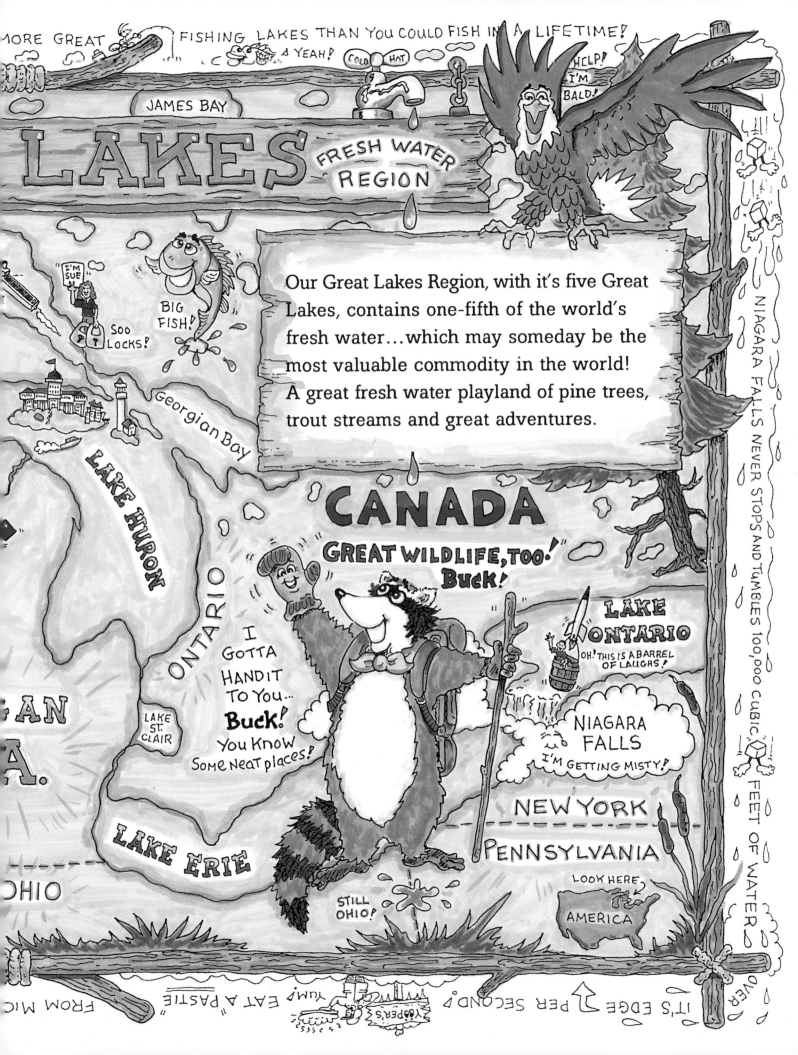

Our Great Lakes Region, with it's five Great Lakes, contains one-fifth of the world's fresh water…which may someday be the most valuable commodity in the world! A great fresh water playland of pine trees, trout streams and great adventures.

The Appalachian Trail is one of the oldest and longest pathways in North America. It extends over 2,000 miles, meandering through river valleys, mountains, 14 states, and 8 national forests. Imagine what our Native Americans and pioneers must have experienced along this scenic trail, which stretches from Maine to Georgia.

Davy Crockett, Daniel Boone, and even secret moonshine stills conjure up images of our Smoky Mountain heritage. Hike the path of history through this part of the Appalachian Mountains. Smell the wild rhododendrons, and enjoy the friendly, resourceful, and hardy people who live here.

Imagine you are a Seminole Indian living in "The Glades" of low mangrove keys and tall sawgrass marshes when the first Spanish explorers appear! This part of our country is always intriguing, just like the Spanish moss that hangs from the trees. Be careful not to disturb nature.

The Grand Canyon is the most spectacular canyon in the world. Some parts of it are over one mile deep! While hiking there, see how the different layers of granite, limestone, sandstone, and shale change color throughout the day.

Glacier National Park is called "the crown of our continent" because of it's unbelievable natural beauty. Take the "Road to the Sun" and you will see mountain goats, grizzly tracks, breathtaking scenery, and unspoiled serenity. As you travel north into Canada it becomes the Waterton-Glacier International Peace Park.

Yellowstone is the oldest national park in the United States. It's surface is covered with more geysers, sinkholes, and hot springs than any other area of the world. Here you can visit the largest wildlife preserve on our continent, so be sure to bring your camera!

ALASKA AND

ALPENGLOW A REFLECTIVE LIGHT SHOW!

I'M FLYING!

WELCOME Buck!

OUR LARGEST STATE ALASKA

SEWARD'S FOLLY WAS OUR COUNTRY'S BIGGEST GAIN!

CONNECTED...$E=MC^2$.

BUCK WILDER

The Alaskan Highway, migrating whales, and "Call of the Wild" all conjure up pictures of our great Yukon Territory. A fly-in fishing trip into Canada, including a shore lunch of freshly-caught walleye and ending with a bird's eye view of the magnificent "Northern Lights," result in some of life's greatest moments.

All park rangers, like "Officer Friendly", can be extremely helpful and informative to hikers and campers. The campground office and rangers can supply you with invaluable information regarding camp locations, fire conditions, and the best places to hike and fish. Please remember to be polite and courteous to everyone you meet.

PICKING A CAMPSITE

When picking a campsite, look first for comfort and safety. Next consider the natural beauty of the spot. Look for clear, high, dry ground away from dead trees and branches that might come down in a storm. Nearby access to water helps a lot when it comes to washing and cleaning.

Check the area for beehives, hornet nests, or big ant mounds. Try to stay away from marshes, wetlands, or stagnant water because of all the bugs and mosquitoes. Face your tent opening toward the best view…generally toward the south for the morning sun and warmth.

PITCHING A TENT

Always try to "pitch a tent" on high and dry ground. Avoid gullies, river basins, and water run-off areas. Leave a little slack in the tent so it doesn't rip when drying.

Clean the ground real smooth under the tent sites. Remove all stones, rocks, and twigs so that the ground is more comfortable to sit and sleep on. If camping under a tree, check for beehives and dead limbs that might be ready to fall.

WHOOO'S OUT THERE!

I LIKE CHOCOLATE MOOSE!

WELCOME BUCK AND RASCAL

I'LL STAKE MY REPUTATIO ON BUCK'S CAMPING ABILITY!

LOOKS LIKE DEER IN THE ARE

BUILDING A CAMPFIRE

Always utilize an existing campsite and campfire pit whenever possible. If none exists and you have to build your own, start by first clearing the ground of all sticks, branches, and any ignitable material. Make a circle of large stones or rocks, which will help contain your fire and define your "fire pit".

Start your fire by lighting small twigs and branches (in a small tepee shape), then keep adding larger dry wood to it. It takes at least 3 logs to build a large fire. Hardwoods have fewer sparks and give off more heat (b.t.u.'s). Clear the grass and twigs from at least 12" around the edge of your "fire pit".

BUCK, I'VE GOT THE MARSHMALLOW STICKS READY!

MARSHMALLOWS
U·TOAST·UM
CREAMY DELIGHTS!

WATER

3. COOKING FIRE

FROM A LAKE OR STREAM —

BECAUSE THEY CONTAIN WATER AND....

MAY

WHEN HEATED, BIRCH BARK FROM DEAD BIRCH TREES LIGHTS FASTER THAN

PAPER - USE IT FOR STARTING YOUR CAMPFIRES. A GREAT CAMPFIRE

Cooking a meal over an open campfire can be one of your most pleasurable outdoor experiences. The aroma of fried potatoes and freshly caught fish cooking over the campfire grill will become a memory worth cherishing. No matter what you are cooking, take the time to enjoy the experience.

Try to cook over the hot coals instead of the open flame, where there is a greater chance of burning your food. A portable metal grate is perfect to cook on, since it is fairly safe and allows you to cook more than one food at a time.

Mosquitoes, flies, ants, and all of those "itchy things" are as much a part of Mother Nature as you and me. They can be a nuisance, but by utilizing protective clothing, repellents, and proper identification you can hike and camp in harmony with them all. Learn how to identify and treat some of those "itchy tormentors" such as poison ivy and poison oak.

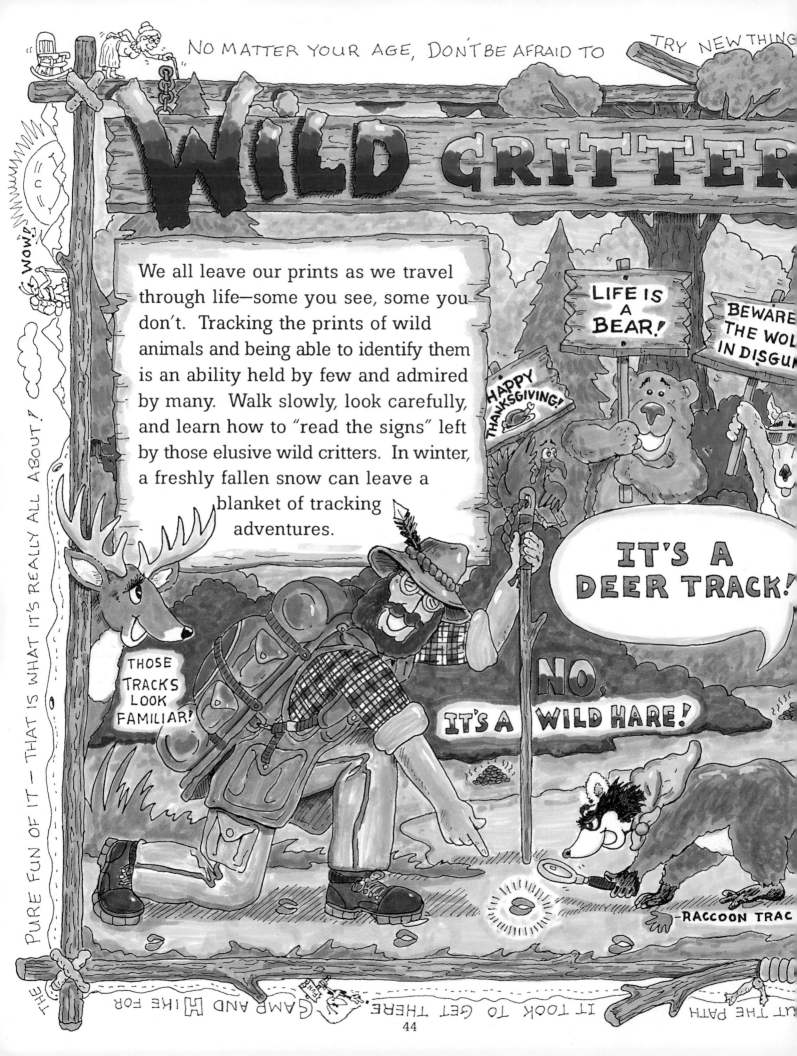

SURVIVAL AND

IT'S FUN TO MAKE UP A....
FIRST AID KIT

A clear freezer bag with a re-sealable top makes a perfect first aid pouch. All of the following items are important to have, depending on the type of hiking/camping trip you are planning.

NEEDLE · BANDAGES · MOLESKIN · STERILE GAUZE · TWEEZERS · UTILITY KNIFE · ELASTIC WRAP · BEE PASTE · BAKING SODA AND WATER · SOAP DISINFECTANT · TOPICAL ANTIBIOTIC · ADHESIVE TAPE · ASPIRIN

PLUS

whistle	insect repellent
extra matches	poison ivy/oak cream
emergency phone numbers	sunscreen
snake bite kit	sunglasses
tick release	money
water purifier	lip balm

OWWOOOO · OWWOOOO · OWWWOOOOOOOOO

HIKING and CAMPING GUIDE

THERE THEY AR... GOODTHING BU... TOLD US WHIC... DIRECTION T... WERE HEADI...

IF NE... LIGHT A

THE LIBRARY IS A GREAT SOURCE FOR SURVIVAL TECHNIQUES — INCLUDING DAILY SURVIVAL?

BUILD CONFIDENCE WHEN DEALING WITH MOTHER NATURE? · TECHNIQUES CAN HELP

"I ROCK AND RULE?"

Carrying a first aid kit and being prepared for the unexpected are two of the best preparations you can make when visiting our great outdoors. Accidents do happen, so learn how to treat and care for some of the most common "field injuries" such as a sprained ankle, cut skin, or a fire burn. Always be prepared!

47

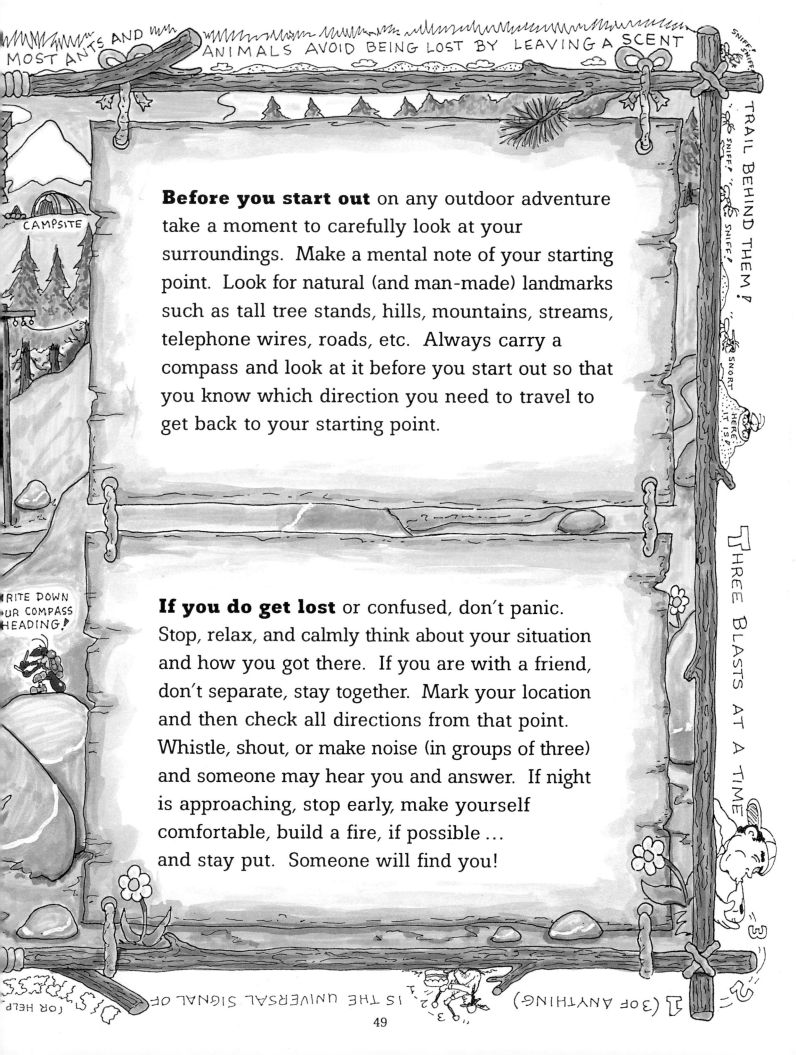

CAMPSITE

Before you start out on any outdoor adventure take a moment to carefully look at your surroundings. Make a mental note of your starting point. Look for natural (and man-made) landmarks such as tall tree stands, hills, mountains, streams, telephone wires, roads, etc. Always carry a compass and look at it before you start out so that you know which direction you need to travel to get back to your starting point.

RITE DOWN
UR COMPASS
HEADING!

If you do get lost or confused, don't panic. Stop, relax, and calmly think about your situation and how you got there. If you are with a friend, don't separate, stay together. Mark your location and then check all directions from that point. Whistle, shout, or make noise (in groups of three) and someone may hear you and answer. If night is approaching, stop early, make yourself comfortable, build a fire, if possible … and stay put. Someone will find you!

THREE BLASTS AT A TIME

WINTER HIKING

SURVIVAL SNOW SHELTER BUILT BY BUCK AND RASCAL!

Buck Book

SPACE BLANKET

MAT

Winter hiking and camping is for the much more rugged and hardy soul. It can be both an adventurous yet a very peaceful experience. Always be prepared for the unexpected and make sure you have plenty of warm, dry gear. Take safety precautions to protect yourself against frostbite or hypothermia (freezing)!

SNOW! REMEMBER TO NEVER EAT YELLOW BRRRR! YOUR HEAT LOSS GOES OUT THROUGH YOUR HEAD.

KEEP YOUR HEAD COVERED BECAUSE MOST BREATHABILITY? WARMTH AND

To have a successful outdoor experience doesn't mean you always have to "rough it." There are many "modern" ways to enjoy our great outdoors. To get the most out of your outdoor experience, though, leave all that city stuff behind.

As the day draws to an end, you can look forward to some wonderful nighttime activities—looking for that first star in the sky, toasting campfire marshmallows, story telling, or maybe even a sing-a-long. Your imagination will sit by the fire with American Indians, fur-capped pioneers, and six-gun cowboys. Just imagine what their stories must have been like.

LET'S SING THE
BUCK WILDER SONG!

Verse: *Hiking and camping,*
Having fun and feeling free.
Follow'n the rules of the great outdoors
Buck Wilder taught to me.

Chorus: *Buck Wilder, Buck Wilder,*
He's the greatest outdoor guy.
Buck Wilder, Buck Wilder,
Says give outdoors a try!

Try to leave your campsite a little cleaner and better organized than when you found it…maybe even stack some wood for the next camper! Remember: what you pack in, you pack out. That means don't leave any paper, plastic, food scraps or anything behind.

Before you "break camp", make sure your fire is completely out. You should be able to run your fingers through the ashes and feel absolutely no heat. If needed, use dirt or lots of water to smother all those cinders.

GLEANING AND S

Get prepared for your next outdoor experience by cleaning and storing your equipment. Wash your cooking utensils, air out your sleeping bag, and dry all clothing and equipment. It helps to label the contents of each of your boxes and containers.

· BUCK WILDER'S ·
RULES TO HIKE AND CAMP BY:

1. **Pack (prepare) at least one day in advance.**
Put all your hiking and camping gear out at least one day before your trip—fishing gear, binoculars, camera, garbage bags, toothpaste, repellents, etc.

2. **Expect the unexpected.**
(Scout motto—Be Prepared!) Rainy days, cold weather, cuts, burns, bee stings.

3. **Pack a First Aid Kit.**
Know how to use it! Include a firestarter, a whistle, and a compass.

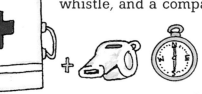

MATCHES

4. **Tell someone where you are going and how long you will be gone.**

CAMPING IN THE BACKYARD... BE HOME TONIGHT FOR DINNER!

5. **Protect Yourself.**
Bring insect repellent, sunscreen, soap, toothpaste, and personal items.

I should have used sunscreen!

6. **Try not to get lost.**
Pay attention to landmarks such as telephone lines, roads, two-tracks, and rivers. Use your compass and mark your location before you start.

MAP

7. If you do get lost.
Don't panic—stay calm. If totally confused, stay where you are and make yourself comfortable. Prepare before dark. Searchers will find you.

WHISTLE

8. Better safe than sorry.
Use extra caution around fires, axes, knives, matches, and hooks.

9. Leave no trace.
Try to leave no sign that you were ever there.

(Pack it in–Pack it out!)

TRASH BAG

10. Get ready for the next adventure.
Clean your equipment, air things out, and get ready to go again.

AIR

CAMPING SUPPLIES

Help our Earth
Pick up trash left by others, pick bottles out of the river, and plant some trees. Do more than your share to help clean up our Earth and to protect our wilderness.

LAST OR FIRST!

RULES

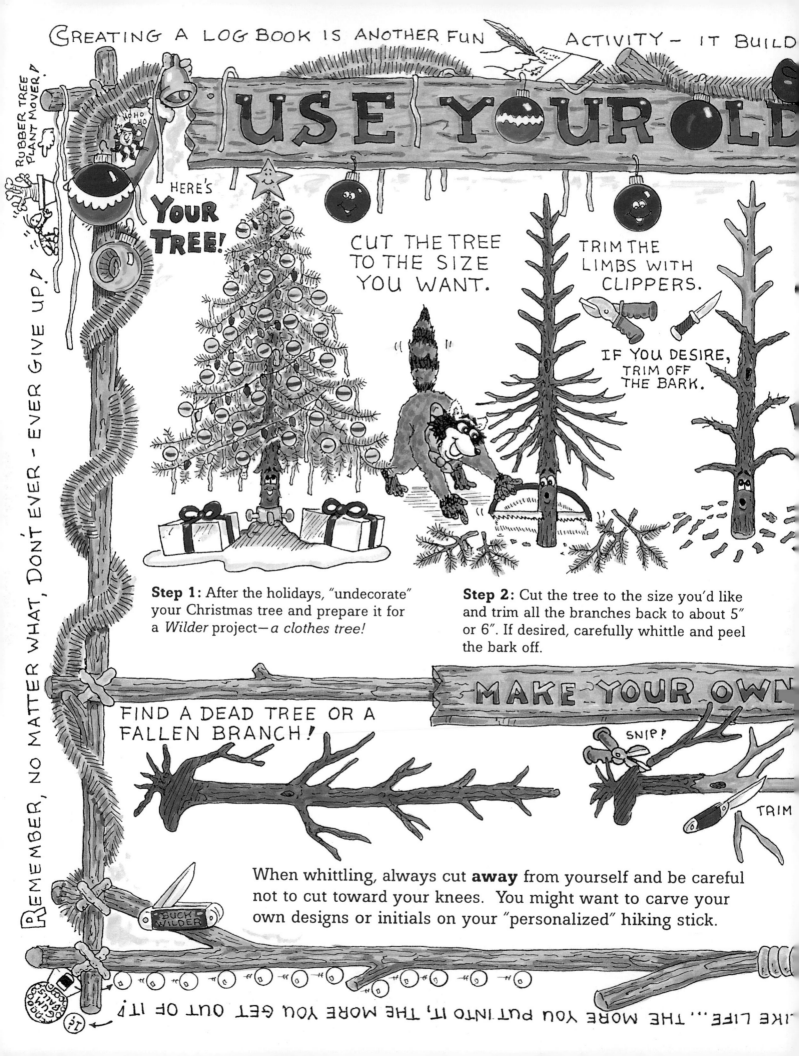

USE YOUR OLD

HERE'S YOUR TREE!

CUT THE TREE TO THE SIZE YOU WANT.

TRIM THE LIMBS WITH CLIPPERS.

IF YOU DESIRE, TRIM OFF THE BARK.

Step 1: After the holidays, "undecorate" your Christmas tree and prepare it for a *Wilder* project—*a clothes tree!*

Step 2: Cut the tree to the size you'd like and trim all the branches back to about 5" or 6". If desired, carefully whittle and peel the bark off.

MAKE YOUR OWN

FIND A DEAD TREE OR A FALLEN BRANCH!

SNIP!

TRIM

When whittling, always cut **away** from yourself and be careful not to cut toward your knees. You might want to carve your own designs or initials on your "personalized" hiking stick.

RUBBER TREE PLANT MOVER?

HO HO HO

BUCK WILDER

REMEMBER, NO MATTER WHAT, DON'T EVER – EVER GIVE UP!

LIKE LIFE... THE MORE YOU PUT INTO IT, THE MORE YOU GET OUT OF IT!

CHRISTMAS TREE

Step 3: Find a block of wood or a stump that needs cutting… one large enough to hold your tree. With a wood chisel, cut a hole the same size as your tree base (you may need some help with this task).

Step 4: Use wood glue to adhere the tree to the base, add screws from the bottom if necessary, and then cover the entire tree with two coats of polyurethane. Let dry and hang your stuff on it… your own **"Buck Rack"**!

HIKING STICK

CARVE YOUR OWN HEAD AND THEN WRAP THE GRIP!

Hiking sticks are perfect for crossing streams, adding support while hiking, and great for poking at mushrooms!

If you would like to order another copy of this book to give as a gift or would like to purchase a copy of *Buck Wilder's Small Fry Fishing Guide* (a complete introduction to the world of fishing for small fry of all ages) just call 1-800-994-BUCK.